Ella Bella Banana's First Most Wonderful World Adventures

by ML Kenofsky

Book Title: Ella Bella Banana's First Most Wonderful World Adventures
Written by ML Kenofsky
Photographs and illustrations by ML Kenofsky
Book design by Heartstone House

Published By: EBB Publications, ellabellabanana.com
Softcover: 979-8-9869757-0-2
Ebook: 979-8-9869757-1-9
Hardcover: 979-8-9869757-2-6

Dedication

To Dr. Kristin MacDonald, Veterinary Cardiologist, and her VCA team, without whose expertise, experience, and compassion, Ella Bella Banana would not be traveling the world.

Acknowledgments

This book could not have been created without the support of many, to whom I'm ever grateful: Robin Hardman for her invaluable editing expertise and ever-appreciated friendship, Nathan Lomas for his expert Photoshop tweaks and guidance, Stuart Schwartz's indispensable encouragement and suggestions, members of Image Flow's Personal Project's class for their helpful comments and photographic inspiration, Tom and Erin Lyons for their invaluable comments and suggestions, Karen Duffy for her love and encouragement, Poem Cusick and Waylynn and Virgil Roberts for their enthusiastic beta testing, Arden Haggin for her tech creativity and help, Bryony van der Merwe for turning a pile of photos and words into a beautiful finished product, and, of course, Ella Bella Banana, who patiently tolerated being wrapped in scarves, adorned in wacky hats, and forced to sit still for one more photo when all she wanted was to play with her toys.

Further thanks to Freepik for the map on pages 8-9, designed by Freepik (www.freepik.com), and to David Iliff, whose photograph of Buckingham Palace on p.18 (LICENSE: CC BY-SA.3.0) was generously made available for free use per the photographer's written instructions and conditions. The photo was cropped by me.

Time for
some fun!

Hi, everybody!

I'm Ella Bella Banana. I love napping on my mom's soft, furry bed and sniffing an occasional butt.

But I also LOVE to travel the world.

Do you want to come with me as I begin my First Most Wonderful World Adventure?!!

Come on! Let's go!

Look at the map on the next page to see where we're heading.

CANADA
San Francisco
UNITED STATES OF AMERICA
Havana, Cuba
MEXICO
CUBA
VENEZUELA
GUYANA
SURINAME
COLOMBIA
ECUADOR
PERU
Peru
BRAZIL
LD MAP
BOLIVIA
PARAGUAY
CHILE
URUGUAY
ARGENTINA

Iceland
London
Prague
Paris
Venice
Morocco
Egypt
ICELAND
FAROE ISLANDS
SWEDEN
FINLAND
NORWAY
LATVIA
BELARUS
GERMANY
UKRAINE
MOLDOVA
FRANCE
KAZKAHSTAN
SPAIN
PORTUGAL
ITALY
TURKEY
UZBEKISTAN
TURKMENISTAN
SYRIA
IRAQ
IRAN
AFGHANISTAN
KASHMIR
PAKISTAN
MOROCCO
ALGERIA
LIBYA
EGYPT
SAUDI ARABIA
OMAN
WESTERN SHARAH
MAURITANIA
MALI
NIGER
CHAD
SUDAN
ERITREA
YEMEN
SENEGAL
THE GAMBIA
BURKINA FASO
GUINEA
NIGERIA
ETHIOPIA
CENTRAL AFRICAN REPUBLIC
SOUTH SUDAN
COTE D'IVOIRE
GHANA
LIBERIA
CAMEROON
SOMALIA
UGANDA
KENYA
GABON
CONGO
DEMOCRATIC REPUBLIC OF THE CONGO
TANZANIA
ANGOLA
ZAMBIA
MOZAMBIQUE
ZIMBAWE
MADAGASCAR
NAMIBIA
BOTSWANA
SOUTH AFRICA
SOUTH
TLANTIC

I'm starting my adventure on the California coast, near San Francisco, where the Pacific Ocean's waves pound onto huge rocks.

The water is soooo cold!

After a few days of warming up on land, I'm heading somewhere tropical.

I'm in Havana, Cuba!

There are lots of beautiful old American cars from the 1950s. I even get to ride in one.

All over Cuba, people sit in the parks or on the street and play dominos. It's the national game.

Can you see me?

LET'S GO!

I'm liking this warm weather, so I think I'll go even further south to South America.

I'm in Peru!

There are lots of Peruvian llamas and alpacas here. (They are related to camels.) Long ago, llamas and alpacas were used to carry supplies across the Andes mountains. When alpacas' fur grows long, people can cut and weave it to make soft sweaters. Llamas are similar to alpacas but are a lot bigger. Don't get too close to either of them because they can spit up to 15 feet! And it stinks!

I think I'd better get out of here before I get spit on! Time to head in a completely different direction...

NORTH...

Do you know where I am?

Iceland is the land of waterfalls, rainbows, and volcanos. Do you like my Viking hat? I've always wanted to be a 'shieldmaiden' (that's a female Viking warrior!).

All over Iceland, there are hot thermal pools - like ponds or lakes - heated by volcanic gasses that bubble up from deep in the earth. Every town has its own pool. The warm water feels so good!

After I shake myself dry, I'll be heading to

mainland Europe.

Hello from

LONDON

England!

I'm in front of the beautiful Buckingham Palace, where the King of England does much of his work. It is guarded by the King's Guard, who are dressed in red coats and bearskin hats.

I stop by the National Portrait Gallery and see a painting that reminds me of someone...

Okay, now let's head off to Prague,

the capital of the Czech Republic.

Prague's churches are beautiful.

This doorway at Vysehrad is decorated with thousands of mosaic tiles.

We're having a snowstorm!

I'm wearing my warmest hat on the famous Charles Bridge in Prague. All the statues along the sides of the bridge are white with snow.

Brrr, time to fly to Paris!

Bonjour!

Welcome to Paris, France!

This baguette (French bread) will make a delicious lunch.

When I'm in Paris, I like to dress up a little because everyone is so fashionable.

Are you ready to visit somewhere very different? A place with no cars...

I'm in Venice, Italy!

Venice has canals instead of roads. No cars or even bicycles. You have to walk or take boats everywhere. Even the taxis and ambulances are boats. Do you think you would like to travel by boat everywhere?

Each morning in Venice, I look out the window to see who is floating by. Sometimes they even wave at me.

In winter, floods (acqua alta) from the Adriatic Sea fill up Saint Mark's Square (Piazza San Marco). I put on tall boots and have so much fun splashing around in the water!

Now it's time to get dry and head to...

Morocco!

Can you find Morocco on the map?

I'm visiting my Berber friend, Idir, in the Moroccan Sahara Desert. He and his family live in tents and move from place to place. They are nomads.

Sunset in the Moroccan Sahara Desert is orange, pink, and purple. Here, I'm dressed in one of the blue robes the men of the Tuareg tribe wear to protect themselves from the sun and sand.

After a fun visit with Idir and his family, I want to see some ancient civilizations.

So I'm flying off to...

Egypt!

The Great Sphinx (a stone-carved statue of a lion with a human head) guards the Great Pyramids of Giza in Egypt. The pyramids were built as tombs for Egypt's pharaohs (kings). Can you tell which one is the real Sphinx?

I don't know why the camel sitting at the Great Pyramid has started yelling, but I decide to yell too!

The sailboats on the Nile River are called feluccas.

This man is our sailboat captain.

DID YOU KNOW that the Nile is the longest river in the world?

Well, it's time to head home to take a long nap before I plan my next most wonderful world adventure. Thanks for joining me! I hope I'll see you again - I've got some great ideas for other fun places to visit.

Your friend,

Ella Bella Banana

About the Author

ML Kenofsky is Ella Bella Banana's Lady-In-Waiting, tending to her canine princess's culinary, medical, travel planning, and personal care needs. It's a full-time job, not unlike tending to the royal family of England.

She and Ella Bella Banana live on the west coast of America and enjoy watching surfers, making art, and, of course, having adventures all over the world.

She can be found online at www.ellabellabanana.com or ellabellabananabooks@gmail.com

A Word from the Author

If you enjoyed this book, it would be wonderful if you could leave a lovely review on Amazon. Your kind feedback is important and very much appreciated.

Thank you so much!